SPOILED A$$ KIDZ!

HOME HAPPY HOUR RECIPES FOR THE FAMILY

Food Allergy Disclaimer:

This book includes a collection of recipes and is written and produced for informational purposes only. BHE LLC does not provide medical or legal advice. BHE LLC does not guarantee that the ingredients listed in any of the recipes are allergy free. If you have a food allergy, you should determine whether you are allergic to the ingredients in each recipe and not rely on statements that a particular recipe is gluten free, dairy free, nut free, soy free, or free of any other possible allergen. Always follow safe food handling guidelines when preparing food. BHE LLC is not a certified dietician or nutritionist. Everyone's dietary needs and restrictions are unique to the individual. You are ultimately responsible for all decisions pertaining to your health.

Bird House Publishing rev date 03/07/21

Contents

ABOUT THE AUTHOR

 I'm Tristeon Moore, a husband and father to two beautiful children, Channing and Parker. By day, I'm a businessman, but at home, my alter ego, the self-taught chef Emeril DeLaGhetto, steals the show in the kitchen!

During the COVID quarantine that began in 2020, I had to create a way for my kidz to have fun and memorable experiences while being stuck in the house. My kidz are what some people would call spoiled. By some people I mean me, but my mom just says they're blessed. They travel the world, enjoy fine dining, and get to do many things I couldn't do until I was an adult. I wanted them to continue having new culinary experiences, so I came up with a Kidz Happy Hour that I began to host for my kidz and their cousins every Friday.

During Kidz Happy Hour, I create delicious mocktails and appetizers for the kidz to enjoy. This has allowed the kidz to continue experiencing new things and have memories they will cherish forever while stuck in our bubble of safety.

I'm a proud Texas native who is currently parked in the San Francisco Bay Area, so my style of cooking is southern soul food at the core. Throughout my traveling, I've learned to appreciate other cultures and learned to recreate dishes from all over. This book is to empower everyone who feels like they can't or don't know how to cook. There is nothing more rewarding than the feeling you get from your family enjoying your creations in the kitchen. I hope you feel that joy as you experience this book!

ABOUT THIS BOOK

I want to take this time to thank all of the readers of this cookbook. This cookbook is designed to be an experience with family and friends. I love to create these dishes and serve my family as if they are at a restaurant. You may want to have your family join you in the kitchen and create these drinks and dishes together as a team. As long as you are having fun and creating memories that last a lifetime with these recipes, you are doing it right!

Tips for reading the recipes:

Always look at your ingredients list and gather all of your ingredients so you can see and touch everything needed in the recipe prior to cooking. The last thing you want to do is start cooking and figure out something is missing and have to do a store run.

Next, read the creation and notes section of the recipe in entirety, two to three times, before you begin cooking to gain familiarity with the cooking process. I like to read over the recipe the day before I make a dish. This may sound like a lot, but, in my experience, it helps you to not miss steps, and it reduces mistakes. Some recipes have ingredients and items that can be made in advance. I make sure to make my notes visible so I'll know where they should be applied in my recipes.

Lastly, take your time. The estimated time on recipes is calculated with everything going right with someone familiar with the recipe. You may take longer to chop veggies, squeeze out fresh juice, or crack eggs, and etc. Do not stress yourself out! Complete the recipe at a pace that is comfortable to you. Do you and have fun with it!

ACKNOWLEDGEMENTS

I want to thank my parents, Travis Moore Sr. and Kassandra Harvey, for making me the man I am today. Growing up in an area where I could have easily gone down the wrong path, it was the discipline and values they instilled in me that kept me on the right path. I love y'all!

To my wife and mother of my two heartbeats, Rachelle, for your continued support and partnership. It was this woman who expanded my palette by exploring other cultures and embracing culinary experiences besides soul food and barbecue. I love you!

To my kidz for motivating me and keeping me on my toes. They put in just as much energy into creating this book as I did. Daddy loves you!

To my Grandfather, Calvin Conerly a.k.a. Big Daddy, for making it look cool to be a man in the kitchen. Love you Big Daddy and Gran!

To my nieces, Delana and Deanna for being my first customers. Thank you! Love, Uncle Tris!

To all of my family and friends who have supported me and constantly pushed me to share my cooking creations with the world. I finally listened! Special shout out to Tinnell for specifically telling me to create cookbooks and giving me the game. To Jamaal for being my kitchen mentor and sparring partner. I love you all.

To my photography team, Korise and Karen Jubert of Town Futurist Media. It was a pleasure collaborating with you, family.

To my publisher Jai Collier and Bird House Publishing, thank you for all of your help, hard work, and guidance in my debut project. I appreciate and thank everyone behind the scenes that had a hand in the creation of this cookbook. I look forward to working with you all again on the next project!

COMMON ABBREVIATIONS
FOR COOKING MEASUREMENTS

Abbreviation (s)	What It Stands For
C, c	cup
gal	gallon
L, l	liter
	pound
mL, ml	milliliter
Oz.	ounce
	pint
qt	quart
t, tsp	teaspoon
T, TB, Tbl, Tbsp	tablespoon

COMMON CONVERSION MEASUREMENTS FOR COOKING

Unit of Measurement:	Equivalent:
Pinch	less than 1/8 teaspoon
3 teaspoons	1 tablespoon
2 tablespoons	1 fluid ounce
4 tablespoons	1/4 cup
5 tablespoons plus 1 teaspoon	1/3 cup
12 tablespoons	3/4 cup
16 tablespoons	1 cup
1 cup	8 fluid ounces
1 Pint	16 fluid ounces
1 quart	32 fluid ounces
4 quarts	1 gallon

HAPPY
HOUR 1

CARMEL MINT CREAM SODA FLOATS &

BBQ CHEDDAR BURGER SLIDERS

Spoiled A$$ Kidz!

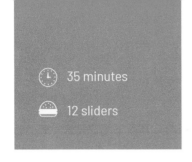

35 minutes

12 sliders

BBQ CHEDDAR BURGER SLIDERS

1 pack of bacon

2 pounds ground beef

1 tablespoon salt

½ tablespoon pepper

1 teaspoon onion powder

1 teaspoon garlic powder

1 tablespoon Worcestershire sauce

6-8 slices cheddar cheese

12 dinner rolls or Hawaiian sweet rolls

1 cup of your favorite barbecue sauce

2 tablespoons butter, melted

CREATION

Preheat the oven to 350°F.

1. Line a baking sheet with foil. Place uncooked bacon on the baking sheet and cook for 20-25 minutes, flipping after 15 minutes. Bacon should be cooked but not crispy because it will cook more, later in the recipe. Once done, remove the bacon from the oven.

2. While the bacon cooks, combine ground beef, salt, pepper, onion powder, garlic powder, and Worcestershire sauce in a 9x13-inch baking dish, mixing thoroughly to combine the ingredients evenly.

3. Press beef flat into a single layer. Bake for 20 minutes. Drain and pat dry with a paper towel. Remove the beef from the baking dish and set it to the side.

4. Slice the whole loaf of rolls in half to create one hamburger bun top and one hamburger bun bottom. Place the bottom half in the baking dish. Place the cooked beef on the bottom sliced bun and spread the barbecue sauce on top of the beef evenly.

5. Top with the sliced cheese then the cooked bacon.

6. Add the top buns and brush with melted butter. Bake for 15-18 minutes, or until the bread is golden brown and the cheese is melted.

Notes

• When cooking the ground beef patty, use a meat thermometer to check the temperature at the 15-minute mark before returning to the oven. For medium beef, the internal temperature should be 140°-145° and slightly pink throughout. Once the meat reaches that temperature, remove from the oven. Remember it will cook for another 15 minutes, later in the recipe, and will cook closer to medium-well (150°- 155°F) or well-done (160° to 165°F). The closer to well-done, the drier your burger will be. For a juicy burger, aim for medium-well.

• For a softer top bun, place the burger patty, cheese, and bacon on the bottom bun and place in the oven for the first 5-7 minutes. Remove the dish from the oven, add the top buns, and return to the oven for the remainder of the time, or until you've reached your desired top bun texture.

Spoiled A$$ Kidz!

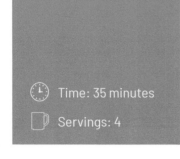

Time: 35 minutes

Servings: 4

CARAMEL MINT CREAM SODA FLOATS

2 liters of cream soda (or your favorite brand of root beer)

2 quarts vanilla gelato or ice cream

1 stalk fresh mint leaves

1 bottle of squeezable caramel syrup

4 servings of your favorite chocolate bar

CREATION

1. Place the serving glasses in the fridge to chill (this helps keep the drink chilled longer).

2. Place 1-2 mint leaves in a glass along with a splash of cream soda.

3. Muddle the mint leaves for 10 seconds then remove with a spoon and discard.

4. Add 2 scoops of vanilla gelato into the glass and squeeze caramel syrup on top.

5. Slowly pour cream soda into the glass until it reaches close to the brim.

6. Add a straw followed by a half scoop of ice cream and place a candy bar directly on top (this will prevent the candy bar from sinking to the bottom of the float).

7. Drizzle with more caramel syrup and garnish with a fresh mint leaf on top.

Serve and enjoy. Cheers!

Notes

• Keep in mind the float is the star of the show. Make sure your candy bar is not too large in size that it takes up too much space in the cup.

Parents Pour: To make this mocktail into a cocktail, add your alcohol of choice prior to the last scoop of ice cream. Try 2 oz. of vanilla-flavored vodka. For those who prefer whiskey, like me, add 1 oz. of bourbon cream and 2 oz. of rye whiskey or bourbon. Cheers!

HAPPY
HOUR 2

FROZEN STRAWBERRY AGAVE VIRGIN MARGARITAS & WONTON TACO CUPS

WONTON TACO CUPS

2 teaspoons olive oil

1 pound ground beef

1 pack carne asada taco seasoning

1 (10 oz.) can of mild diced tomatoes and green chilies, drained

24 wonton wrappers

1 pack of Mexican blend cheese

non-stick cooking spray

Topping Options

sour cream

guacamole

green onions, sliced

fresh tomatoes, diced

jalapenos

lettuce, shredded

salsa

taco sauce

CREATION

Preheat the oven to 400°F.

1. Heat the olive oil in a large skillet over medium-high heat.

2. Add ground beef to the skillet, stirring continuously and breaking the meat up into crumbles.

3. Add the taco seasoning. Cook the meat for another 4-5 minutes or until there is no pink.

4. Stir in the canned tomatoes and chilies.

5. Coat a 12-cup muffin tin with cooking spray. Place one wonton wrapper into the bottom of each muffin cup.

6. Spoon 1 tablespoon of cooked meat into each cup and top with a tablespoon of cheese.

7. Place a second wonton layer on top of the first layer of meat and cheese and lightly press down to create another bowl-like area, then repeat to add a second layer of meat and cheese onto each wonton. To create a gorgeous flower illusion, make sure the points of the wontons are placed in opposite directions.

8. Bake for 8-12 minutes or until edges are browned and cheese is melted.

9. Top each taco cup with your choice of toppings that make your kidz happiest.

Serve and enjoy!

Notes

• These taco cups are fun because you can dress them up with a multitude of variations. Grab the taco ingredients that your kidz love the most and top accordingly. These can be unique to everyone!

4

5 minutes

FROZEN STRAWBERRY AGAVE MARGARITAS

2 cups frozen strawberries

6 oz. orange juice, freshly squeezed

4 oz. lime juice, freshly squeezed

4 oz. agave nectar

1 oz. orange blossom water

4 oz. simple syrup

2 ½ cups ice

1 tablespoon sugar

Garnish

4 fresh strawberries

1 lime, juiced

4 lime rounds, sliced

¼ sugar for glass rim

CREATION

1. In a blender, combine all ingredients and blend until smooth.

Garnishing

Pour lime juice on a plate. On another plate, pour ¼ cup of sugar.

Dip the rim of each serving glass in the lime juice then dip, spin in the sugar and set aside.

Pour margarita into the sugar-rimmed glass.

Add a slice of lime to the center of the margarita.

Cut a slit into the fresh strawberry and place the slit over the rim of the glass.

Serve and enjoy. Cheers!

Notes

• With frozen drinks, consistency is very important. You don't want your drink too runny because it will melt too fast, but also not so thick that it can't be sipped with a straw. Use a spoon to test the consistency. If it is too thick then you used too much ice. Blend it longer to make it smoother and add a splash more of the liquid ingredients. If it is too thin and watery, add more frozen strawberries and a tad more ice to thicken it.

Parents Pour: Add .5 oz. of orange liqueur and 1.5 oz. of tequila to your drink to remove the word virgin from your version! Cheers!

HAPPY
HOUR 3

MOCKSCOW MULES &

MILLIONAIRE BACON-WRAPPED CHEESE TOTS

Spoiled A$$ Kidz!

5 minutes

24-36 tots

MILLIONAIRE BACON-WRAPPED CHEESE TOTS

1 bag of frozen tater tots, thawed to room temperature

• 1 pack of snack-size cheese squares, individually wrapped

8-12 slices bacon, cut equally into thirds

¼ cup brown sugar, packed

1 cup of sour cream (for dipping)

1 pack of wooden toothpicks

non-stick cooking spray

Garnish

1 green onion, chopped (green part only)

CREATION

Preheat the oven to 400° F.

1. Line a baking sheet with foil, spray with non-stick spray, and set aside.

2. Arrange bacon in pan and evenly coat with brown sugar and press into the bacon. Allow to sit for 10-15 minutes.

3. Cut cheese squares into strips the length and width of a tater tot. Wrap each tater tot with a cheese square strip, followed by a piece of bacon, brown sugar side up (be sure not to wrap too tight so the tater tots won't burst while baking).

4. Gently insert a toothpick into the bacon end piece through each tot, careful not to break the tater tot.

5. Place tater tots onto the prepared baking sheet pan. Place into the oven and bake for 20-25 minutes, flipping each tot halfway through the baking time to ensure they cook evenly.

Garnishing

Sprinkle chopped green onions over the tots after they've finished cooking.

Optional: sprinkle chopped green onion in a cup of sour cream and use it as a dipping sauce.

Serve and enjoy!

Notes

• Consider coating the bacon with the brown sugar the night before to allow the sugar to soak in. If your family enjoys spicy food, adding crushed red pepper flakes to your bacon coating and using a spicy cheese such as pepper jack can take it to the next level.

• Use a firm cheese for this dish. Don't use a soft cheese, like American cheese, because it will melt before the bacon cooks. Also, freezing the cheese prior to wrapping it will slow down the melting process when cooking.

• This dish can be prepared in an air fryer. Reduce the cooking time by 5-10 minutes.

Spoiled A$$ Kidz!

5 minutes

1

MOCKSCOW MULE

crushed ice

- 1 bottle ginger beer

1 oz. lime juice, freshly squeezed

⅓ cup ginger ale

Garnish

fresh mint

1 lime wedge

CREATION

A copper mule mug is traditionally used with this cocktail.

1. Fill cup ⅓ full with ice.
2. Pour in lime juice and ginger ale and fill the cup to top with ginger beer.
3. Stir to combine.

Garnishing

Place a sprig of mint and the lime wedge on top of the drink.

Serve and enjoy. Cheers!

Notes

- Do not let the name mislead you! Ginger beer is non-alcoholic, so this cocktail is safe for kidz.

Parents Pour: To convert this drink into a Moscow Mule, substitute the ⅓ cup ginger ale for 2 oz. of vodka. For a Kentucky Mule, substitute the ⅓ cup ginger ale for 2 oz. of whiskey.

HAPPY
HOUR 4

SPARKLING MINT JULEP MOCKTAIL &
CAJUN SHRIMP JAMBALAYA

1 pound raw shrimp, tail-on, peeled and deveined

1 package of andouille sausage, sliced into rounds

1 pound boneless skinless chicken breasts or thighs, cut into 1-inch pieces

3 cups low sodium chicken broth

2 tablespoons Cajun seasoning

½ tablespoon onion powder

½ tablespoon garlic powder

2 teaspoons smoked paprika

1 onion, diced

1 small green bell pepper, cored & diced

1 small yellow bell pepper, cored and diced

1 small red bell pepper, cored and diced

2 stalks/ribs celery, chopped

4 garlic cloves, minced

1 (14 oz.) can crushed tomatoes

3 teaspoons salt

1 teaspoon ground black pepper

1 teaspoon thyme

1 teaspoon oregano

1 bay leaf

2 teaspoons Worcestershire sauce

3 tablespoons cooking oil, divided

1 ½ cups uncooked white rice

Garnish

1 green onion, chopped

finely chopped parsley

60 minutes

6-8 people

CAJUN SHRIMP JAMBALAYA

Notes

• If you or anyone in your family has a shellfish allergy, prepare the shrimp separately. Season shrimp with Cajun seasonings. Warm olive oil in a separate skillet. Add raw shrimp and cook until the shrimp are cooked through, about 2-3 minutes. Doing this avoids contaminating the entire dish, making it inedible for those with shellfish allergies. Simply add shrimp to the bowls of those who can tolerate it. Serve and enjoy!

• Be careful not to break the bay leaf while stirring. Pieces of that in your dish can be unpleasant.

CREATION

1. Season the chicken pieces with 1 tablespoon of the Cajun seasoning. Set aside.

2. Heat 1 tablespoon of oil in a large pot over medium heat.

3. Brown the sausage in the hot oil. Remove the cooked sausage, leaving the oil in the pot. Add the remainder of the oil to the pot and sauté the chicken until browned. Remove cooked chicken, leaving the oil in the pot. Set aside in the same bowl as the sausage.

4. Sauté the onion, peppers, and celery until the onions are soft and translucent then add the garlic and cook for 30 seconds.

5. Stir in the tomatoes and add the remaining Cajun seasoning, salt, pepper, thyme, oregano, bay leaf, onion powder, garlic powder, smoked paprika, and Worcestershire sauce. Add the chicken and sausage. Cook for 5 minutes, stirring occasionally.

6. Add the rice and chicken broth, bring to a boil, then reduce heat to low-medium. Cover and let simmer for 15 to 20 minutes, or until liquid is absorbed and rice is cooked. Stir regularly and ensure your rice does not stick to the bottom of the pot and your liquid does not dry out before rice finishes cooking (add more broth and adjust stove temperature if needed). Season to taste.

7. Place the shrimp on top of the jambalaya mixture, stir gently, and cover with lid. Allow mixture to simmer while stirring occasionally until the shrimp are cooked through and pink, about 5 minutes (thicker shrimp could require more time).

8. Remove bay leaf prior to serving.

Garnishing

Sprinkle the pot of jambalaya with chopped green onions and finely chopped parsley.

Serve and enjoy!

Spoiled A$$ Kidz!

SPARKLING MINT JUBILEE MOCKTAIL

1 bottle sparkling apple cider

2 cups pineapple juice

1 cup orange juice, fresh (do not use orange juice from concentrate)

¼ cup lemon juice, freshly squeezed

honey brown sugar simple syrup

crushed ice

Garnish

fresh mint

lemon wedges

For the honey brown sugar simple syrup

- ½ cup honey

- ½ cup water

- ¼ cup brown sugar

- Add honey, water, and brown sugar to a saucepan and cook over medium heat until the sugar and honey are dissolved. Remove from heat and place in the fridge to cool.

CREATION

1. In a pitcher, pour sparkling apple cider, pineapple juice, orange juice, lemon juice, and chilled honey brown sugar syrup. Stir to combine.

2. Fill cocktail glasses with ice.

3. Pour the drink over ice.

Garnishing

Place a lemon wedge in the glass. Place a mint sprig in the glass, leaning against the lemon wedge. Pour in the mocktail. Serve and enjoy! Cheers!

Notes

- Honey brown sugar syrup can be made the day of or hours prior to serving the drinks to allow time to cool longer.

Parents Pour

With this mocktail's vibrant flavor, you can't go wrong by adding a shot of your favorite hard liquor to top it off.

HAPPY
HOUR 5

OCEAN WATER &

HONEY GARLIC AIR FRIED CHICKEN WINGS

Spoiled A$$ Kidz!

45 minutes

4-6 people

HONEY GARLIC AIR FRIED CHICKEN WINGS

2 pounds chicken wings

1 tablespoon salt

1 tablespoon coarse black pepper

1 teaspoon ground mustard

1 teaspoon celery seed

1 teaspoon garlic powder

2 tablespoons coconut or olive oil

non-stick cooking spray

Sauce

1 tbsp unsalted butter

4 garlic cloves, peeled and finely minced

1 pinch of salt

1 cup honey

2 teaspoons soy sauce

1 tsp sesame oil

½ oz. orange juice, freshly squeezed

Garnish

green onion, diced

sesame seeds

CREATION

Preheat the air fryer to 390°F.

1. In a bowl, mix all the seasonings until they are well combined.
2. Rinse chicken and pat dry with a paper towel. Toss chicken and coconut oil in a bowl, making sure all pieces are coated, then evenly coat the chicken with the seasonings.
3. Spray the air fryer basket with non-stick cooking spray then transfer the wings to the air fryer basket, being sure not to overcrowd the basket so wings cook evenly.
4. Air fry the wings for 25-35 minutes, turning the chicken every 10 minutes to ensure they are cooking and browning evenly.
5. While wings cook, prepare the honey-garlic sauce. On the stove, heat butter and garlic in a small saucepan over medium-low heat, careful not to brown the garlic. Stir in the honey, soy sauce, sesame oil, orange juice, and salt, stirring constantly until sauce thickens, about 8-10 minutes. Keep warm.
6. Transfer cooked chicken wings to a mixing bowl and pour on a generous amount of honey-garlic sauce, tossing to evenly coat each wing.

Garnishing

Transfer the cooked and coated wings from the mixing bowl to a plate or platter. Sprinkle with sesame seeds and thinly sliced green onions. Serve hot and enjoy!

Notes

• If you do not own an air fryer, no worries! You can prepare this recipe in the oven. Preheat the oven to 425°. Prepare a baking sheet by spraying with non-stick cooking spray. Arrange the seasoned chicken on the baking sheet, spaced so the pieces are not touching. Bake for 40-45 minutes or until chicken is cooked through. Be sure to flip wings half way through time for them to cook evenly.

Spoiled A$$ Kidz!

45 minutes

4

OCEAN WATER

- 48 oz. lemon-lime soda

1 oz. pineapple juice

4 oz. simple syrup

2 teaspoons coconut extract

3 drops blue food coloring

Garnish

fish-shaped chewy candy

cocktail umbrellas

lemon popping candy

lemon slices

ice

CREATION

1. Into a pitcher or punch bowl, pour soda, pineapple juice, simple syrup, and coconut extract. Stir to combine.

2. Add blue food coloring, one drop at a time until you reach your desired ocean color. Stir and mix well.

3. Serve over ice

Garnishing

- Serve in 2 fish bowl cups. Top with 2-3 fish-shaped candies and add a straw and cocktail umbrella.

Serve and enjoy. Cheers!

Notes

- Recipe serves one 12 oz. can per serving. If you prefer, you can purchase a 2-liter bottle of soda instead of a 12-pack of cans.

- If you're not afraid to make a mess, you can have a lot of fun with the kidz with this one! Use lemon popping candy or yellow sugar to create a sand effect for staging the drinks

Parents Pour: To create a cocktail, add 1.5 oz of rum to your glass, as it will marry well with the coconut extract and pineapple juice.

HAPPY
HOUR 6

PURPLE RAIN & SWEET CHILI CHICKEN MEATBALLS

30 minutes

30-40 Meatballs

SWEET CHILI CHICKEN MEATBALLS

non-stick cooking spray

2 pounds ground chicken

4 garlic cloves, minced

1 tablespoon salt

2 teaspoons pepper

½ teaspoon paprika

1 teaspoon onion powder

1 cup crushed crackers or panko breadcrumbs

2 large eggs

1 (10 oz.) bottle sweet chili sauce

Garnish

fresh parsley, finely chopped

toothpicks

CREATION

Preheat the oven to 475ºF.

1. Prepare two baking sheets with foil and spray with non-stick cooking spray.

2. In a large bowl, combine the ground chicken, salt, pepper, paprika, onion powder, crushed crackers (or panko breadcrumbs), and eggs. Use your hands to mix all the ingredients together. Make sure the seasoning is worked in evenly without over mixing, careful not to dry out the mixture.

3. Use an ice cream scoop and gather about 3 tablespoons of the mixture to form your meatballs. Place your round meatballs on the prepared baking pans.

4. Bake meatballs for 10-12 minutes or until completely cooked.

5. Pour half the bottle of your sweet chili sauce in a bowl. Remove cooked meatballs from the oven and brush with sweet chili sauce.

6. Return the pans of meatballs to the oven and bake for an additional 1-2 minutes.

Garnishing

Insert a toothpick into each meatball. Sprinkle with fresh parsley, place on a platter.

Pour the remaining sweet chili sauce in a bowl for dipping.

Serve and enjoy. Cheers!

Notes

• Some sweet chili sauces are more sweet than heat, which my kidz enjoy. For families who want more heat, add crushed red pepper to your chili sauce.

Spoiled A$$ Kidz!

5 minutes

8

PURPLE RAIN

2 cups purple grape juice

2 cups Simply blueberry lemonade

2 scoops vanilla bean gelato or your favorite vanilla ice cream

2 scoops passionfruit sorbet

2 cups ice

1 cup frozen blueberries

Garnish

purple rock candy

blackberries

toothpicks

CREATION

1. Add all ingredients to a blender and mix until well blended.
2. Pour into glasses and top each serving with rock candy.

Serve and enjoy. Cheers!

Notes

• For a healthier garnish, place 3-4 fresh blackberries or blueberries on a toothpick and place across the rim of the glass.

Parents Pour: Transform this mocktail into a cocktail by topping your glass with 1.5 oz. of lemon-flavored vodka and stirring to combine.

HAPPY
HOUR 7

PINK FUZZIES &

BBQ CHICKEN FLATBREAD

Spoiled A$$ Kidz!

30 minutes

4

BBQ CHICKEN FLATBREAD

2 chicken breasts

2 tablespoons olive oil

• 1 family size rectangle flatbread pizza dough

1 teaspoon salt

1 teaspoon pepper

½ teaspoon garlic powder

¼ teaspoon chili powder

1 bottle of your favorite barbecue sauce

1 (16 oz.) bag of shredded Mexican blend cheese

¼ cup red onion, thinly sliced

¼ cup cilantro, finely chopped

non-stick cooking spray

prepared sweet and smoky rub (optional)

CREATION

Prepare a baking pan with cooking spray.

1. Season chicken breasts on both sides with garlic powder, chili powder, salt, and pepper or prepared sweet and smoky rub.

2. Heat olive oil in a pan over the stove and cook chicken over medium heat for 5-6 minutes on each side until cooked thoroughly. Remove from heat and chop chicken into ½ inch pieces.

3. With a spoon, spread ½ cup of barbecue sauce, evenly covering the flatbread. Then evenly cover the flatbread with cheese followed by red onions. Next, top with chicken, another light sprinkle of cheese, and one more drizzle of barbecue sauce in a zig-zag pattern across the flatbread. Lastly, sprinkle the cilantro over the whole pizza.

4. Bake for 10-12 minutes until the cheese is melted and the edges of the flatbread start to brown slightly. Slice the flatbread into even pieces.

Serve and enjoy.

Notes

• If you are having trouble finding the premade flatbread dough, feel free to use the regular round pizza dough. While the shape and presentation may differ, the recipe remains the same.

Spoiled A$$ Kidz!

7 minutes

4

PINK FUZZIES

12 oz. can frozen pink lemonade, concentrated

1 cup vanilla bean gelato or your favorite vanilla ice cream

1 cup frozen strawberries

1 cup crushed ice

12 oz. sparkling white grape juice

Garnish

1 can of whipped cream

fresh strawberries

CREATION

1. Add all of the ingredients to a blender and blend until smooth.

Garnishing

Pour mixture into serving glass. Slice a fresh strawberry from the bottom and place on the rim of the glass. Top the glass with whipped cream.

Serve and enjoy. Cheers!

Parents Pour: To make this into a cocktail, swap the sparkling white grape juice for 12 oz of vodka before blending.

HAPPY
HOUR 8

PINEY PEACH &

CAJUN SALMON ALFREDO CROSTINI

Spoiled A$$ Kidz!

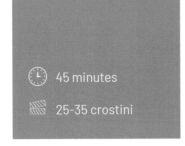

45 minutes

25-35 crostini

CAJUN SALMON ALFREDO CROSTINI

1 pound fresh salmon or any boneless fish

7 tablespoons olive oil, divided (2 oz. for salmon 5 oz. for crostini)

1 lemon

2 teaspoons Cajun seasoning

1 loaf French baguette, cut diagonally into ¼ inch slices

1 pinch oregano

1 pinch basil

1 pinch of salt

non-stick cooking spray

Garnish

sun-dried tomatoes, chopped

fresh parsley, finely chopped

For the Alfredo sauce

½ cup butter

1½ cups heavy whipping cream

4 garlic cloves, minced

½ teaspoon Italian seasoning

1 teaspoon salt

½ teaspoon coarse black pepper

2 cups parmesan cheese

Add the butter and cream to a saucepan. Simmer over low heat for 2 minutes. Stir in the salt, pepper, Italian seasoning, and fresh garlic, and cook for one minute. Add the parmesan cheese, stirring until melted completely.

CREATION

Preheat the oven to 350°F.

1. Prepare a baking pan with non-stick cooking spray.

2. In a small bowl, pour 5 tablespoons of olive oil and add a pinch of salt, oregano, and basil. Stir to combine.

3. Lightly brush each slice of bread with olive oil on both sides and place crostini on a baking pan. Toast in oven until light golden, around 4-5 minutes on each side. Remove from the oven, and place on a wire rack to cool.

4. Rinse salmon and pat dry with a paper towel. Squeeze fresh lemon juice over the salmon and season with Cajun seasoning.

5. Warm a large skillet with oil over medium-low heat. Raise the heat to medium-high. Place the salmon, skin-side up, and cook for 4-5 minutes. Flip fish and cook for another 3 minutes.

6. Transfer fish to a plate to remove the skin, then return the fish to the cooled skillet.

7. Ladle 1 cup of alfredo sauce over the cooked salmon in the pan, and stir the salmon in order to break it apart while letting the alfredo sauce mix in evenly.

8. Place crostini bread on a serving platter. Evenly spoon salmon alfredo on top of crostini, covering each piece.

Garnishing:

• Place chopped sundried tomato over the crostini. Add a dollop of alfredo sauce on top of each crostini, Lastly, sprinkle fresh parsley over the crostini.

Serve and enjoy!

Notes

• This dish is a great chance to get your kidz to step out of their comfort zone and expand their minds when it comes to food. This dish does not lose its appeal without garnishing. If the sundried tomato is too much for your kidz, don't add it to all of the crostini.

Spoiled A$$ Kidz!

5 minutes

1

PINEY PEACH

2.5 oz. peach sparkling
fruit drink

2 oz. pineapple juice

½ oz. lime juice, freshly
squeezed

½ oz. simple syrup

3 dashes orange
blossom water

ice

Garnish

fresh pineapple, sliced

fresh peach slices

CREATION

1. In a cocktail shaker, add ice followed by all ingredients except the peach sparkling fruit drink. Secure the lid of the shaker and vigorously shake for 20 seconds.

2. Remove the top and pour the drink into the glass.

3. Top with the 2.5 oz. of sparkling peach fruit drink and stir to combine.

Garnishing

• Add a slice of pineapple to the rim of the glass. Top beverage with 3 flat slices of peaches.

Serve and Enjoy!

Notes

• If you want to be ambitious with your garnishing, pluck 3 leaves from a pineapple. Cut the top of the pineapple into a half-moon shape. Fill cup with ice and stand the 3 leaves in the glass and secure with sliced pineapple. Pour drink over the ice and top with 3 thin slices of half-moon shaped peaches and serve.

Parents Pour: For a refreshing cocktail creation, add 1.5 oz. of vodka to the drink prior to topping with the 2.5 oz. of peach sparkling fruit drink.

DEDICATION

This book is dedicated to my wife, Rachelle, my spoiled ass kidz, Channing and Parker, and my parents, Travis Moore Sr. and Kassandra Harvey.

For everyone that says they can't cook remember this: a wise man once said if you can dodge traffic then you can dodge a ball. Same thing goes in the kitchen. If you can read a book, then you can cook!

CPSIA information can be obtained
at www.ICGtesting.com
Printed in the USA
BVHW022229130521
607264BV00009B/327